HOW DOES
IT WORK?

How Does a
ROCKET
Work?

BY SARAH EASON

Gareth Stevens
Publishing

Please visit our Web site www.garethstevens.com. For a free color catalog of all our high-quality books, call toll free 1-800-542-2595 or fax 1-877-542-2596.

Library of Congress Cataloging-in-Publication Data
Eason, Sarah.
    How does a rocket work? / Sarah Eason.
      p. cm. -- (How does it work?)
    Includes bibliographical references and index.
    ISBN 978-1-4339-3477-3 (library binding) -- ISBN 978-1-4339-3478-0 (pbk.)
    ISBN 978-1-4339-3479-7 (6-pack)
    1. Rocketry--Juvenile literature. 2. Rockets (Aeronautics)--Juvenile literature. I. Title.
  TL782.5.E24 2010
  629.4--dc22
                                                     2009037155

Published in 2010 by
Gareth Stevens Publishing
111 East 14th Street, Suite 349
New York, NY 10003

© 2010 The Brown Reference Group Ltd.

For Gareth Stevens Publishing:
Art Direction: Haley Harasymiw
Editorial Direction: Kerri O'Donnell

For The Brown Reference Group Ltd:
Editorial Director: Lindsey Lowe
Managing Editor: Tim Harris
Editor: Sarah Eason
Children's Publisher: Anne O'Daly
Design Manager: David Poole
Designer: Paul Myerscough
Production Director: Alastair Gourlay

Picture Credits:
Front cover: Shutterstock: Dimitry Romanchuck (background); Brown Reference Group (foreground)

Illustrations by Roger Wade-Walker and Mark Walker

Picture Credits Key: t – top, b – below, c – center, l – left, r – right. Dreamstime: Joe Mercier 26; NASA: 6, 7, 8, 10, 13, 14, 15t, 15b, 18, 19, 21, 22, 23, 24, 25, 27t, 28, 29; Shutterstock: Mike Norton 17, Stephen Sweet 20; Wikipedia: 27b

Publisher's note to educators and parents: Our editors have carefully reviewed the Web sites that appear on p. 31 to ensure that they are suitable for students. Many Web sites change frequently, however, and we cannot guarantee that a site's future contents will continue to meet our high standards of quality and educational value. Be advised that students should be closely supervised whenever they access the Internet.

Printed in the United States of America
1 2 3 4 5 6 7 8 9   12 11 10

CPSIA compliance information: Batch #BRW0102GS: For further information contact Gareth Stevens, New York, New York at 1-800-542-2595.

Contents

How Does a Shuttle Work?

Giant rockets propel the space shuttle into space. The shuttle then uses small rockets to steer while the spacecraft is in orbit.

The robotic arm releases satellites and other objects into space. It also recovers objects and pulls them into the cargo bay.

The crew controls the robotic arm from this area.

The crew can see outside the shuttle using cameras such as this one.

The crew controls the shuttle from the flight deck during take-off and landing.

The mid-deck is the crew's working and living area.

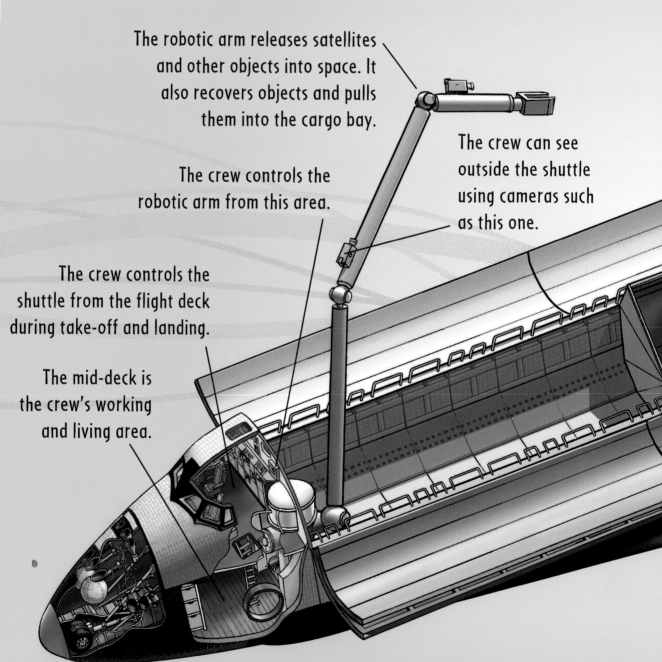

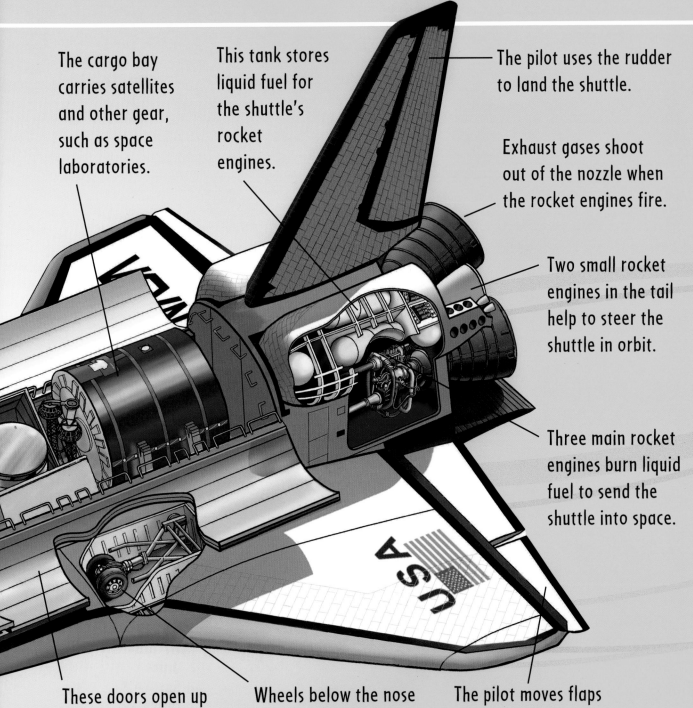

The cargo bay carries satellites and other gear, such as space laboratories.

This tank stores liquid fuel for the shuttle's rocket engines.

The pilot uses the rudder to land the shuttle.

Exhaust gases shoot out of the nozzle when the rocket engines fire.

Two small rocket engines in the tail help to steer the shuttle in orbit.

Three main rocket engines burn liquid fuel to send the shuttle into space.

These doors open up when the shuttle is in orbit so the crew can release satellites and other cargo into space.

Wheels below the nose and each wing lower so the shuttle can land.

The pilot moves flaps called elevons on each wing to land the shuttle.

Rocket History

Over the centuries, rockets have developed from simple fireworks into the rockets that shoot spacecraft into space.

About 1,000 years ago, Chinese scientists invented gunpowder. They used it to make rockets called fireworks. They fired the fireworks to light up the sky during celebrations. They also fired them at their enemies during war. Rockets have been used as weapons ever since. During World War II (1939–1945), the Germans made a rocket-powered bomb, called the V2. Between 1944 and 1945, the Germans fired thousands of V2 rockets, killing many British people.

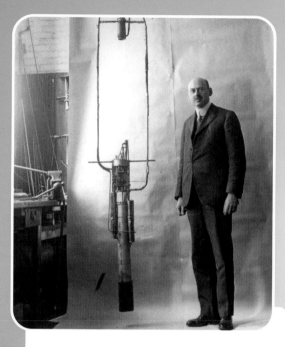

Robert Goddard stands next to one of his liquid-fuel rockets in 1925.

Space rockets

Russian scientist Konstantin Tsiolkovsky (1857–1935) was the first person to think about firing a rocket into space. In the 1920s, his dream turned into reality. U.S. scientist Robert Goddard (1882–1945) invented a rocket powered by liquid fuel instead of gunpowder. His rocket flew

Fun Facts

Between 1967 and 1973, the United States used Saturn V rockets 13 times to send a total of 12 astronauts to the Moon.

faster and farther than any rocket had before.

Space race

After World War II, scientists from the United States and the Soviet Union (now called Russia) wanted to be the first country to send a rocket into space. In 1957, the Soviet Union won the race. They sent the first satellite, *Sputnik 1*, into space aboard a giant rocket. The Soviet Union won another race, too. They used a rocket to send the first person into space in 1961. His name was Yuri Gagarin (1934–1968). U.S. scientists wanted to take control of the space race. During the 1960s, they built a giant rocket, Saturn V, that could fly astronauts to the Moon. They achieved their goal in 1969.

Rockets today

Today, many countries build rockets to send people and spacecraft into space. In the United States, scientists have built the space shuttle. The space shuttle sends satellites into space and carries astronauts to and from space stations.

Edwin "Buzz" Aldrin stands on the Moon. A rocket took the crew of the *Apollo 9* spacecraft there in 1969.

THAT'S AMAZING!

In 1957, the Soviets used a rocket to send a dog called Laika into space. They wanted to check that it was safe for people, too.

Solid Fuel

Fireworks and other simple rockets burn solid fuel. All solid-fuel rockets work in the same way. When the fuel burns, hot exhaust gases escape from the bottom of the rocket. This makes the rocket fly up into the sky.

Gunpowder is a solid fuel. It is a mixture of chemicals that burns very quickly. When it burns, the fuel makes a mixture of hot gases. These gases push out of a tiny hole, called a nozzle, in the bottom of the rocket.

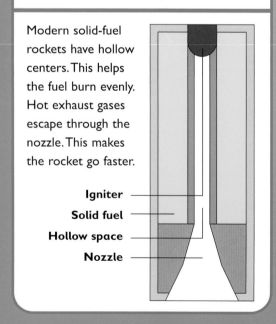

Solid-fuel rocket

Modern solid-fuel rockets have hollow centers. This helps the fuel burn evenly. Hot exhaust gases escape through the nozzle. This makes the rocket go faster.

Igniter
Solid fuel
Hollow space
Nozzle

Solid fuel fills the two huge rockets that send the space shuttle into space.

Why does a rocket fly up?

English scientist Isaac Newton (1642–1727) was the first person to explain how a rocket works. Newton knew that one force produces another force that acts in the opposite direction. So the force of the gases pushing out of the nozzle produces another force that sends the rocket up into the sky.

Early solid-fuel rockets

The first solid-fuel rockets were tubes made of cardboard or paper and filled with gunpowder. A piece of string, called a fuse, stuck out of the rocket's base. Lighting the fuse made the fuel burn. Exhaust gases pushed out of the base of the tube, sending the rocket into the air. These early rockets stood on a long stick. This helped them to fly in a straight line.

Modern solid-fuel rockets

Solid-fuel rockets are still sometimes used today. The space shuttle uses solid-fuel rockets to fly into space. The fuel is a mixture of chemicals that burn much hotter and more quickly. The chemicals are mixed into a paste so they are safe until the rocket is ready to launch.

TRY FOR YOURSELF

Action and reaction

Newton's idea about forces is written down in his third law:

"Every action has an equal but opposite reaction."

You can test this out for yourself.

You will need:
• heavy rock   • skateboard

1 Find an open space with a level surface.
2 Find a large, heavy rock.
3 Stand sideways on a skateboard. Throw the rock to your left, making sure no one is in the way.
4 The force of throwing the rock to the right produces an equal and opposite force. This pushes you and the skateboard to the right.

In a rocket, the action is the force of the gases pushing out of the base of the rocket. The reaction is the force of the rocket flying up into the sky.

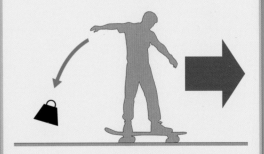

Liquid Fuel

The most powerful rockets use liquid fuels. They are used to send satellites and people into space.

Liquid-fuel rockets are perfect for space travel. They are more powerful, faster, and go farther than solid-fuel rockets.

Liquid or gas?

Liquid fuels are really cold gases stored under pressure. The fuel is actually two liquids: a propellant and an oxidizer. Most liquid-fuel rockets use liquid oxygen as the oxidizer. Different rockets use different propellants. The rockets that launch the space shuttle use liquid hydrogen as the propellant.

Scientists test a liquid fuel rocket before the launch.

Liquid-fuel rocket

Propellant tank

Oxidizer tank

Pump

Fuel injector

Propellant cools combustion chamber and nozzle

Liquids mix together

This diagram shows how a liquid-fuel rocket works.

Exhaust gases

In the mix

The oxidizer and propellant are stored in separate tanks. The liquids mix and burn in a combustion chamber. Very hot exhaust gases then shoot out of the nozzle. This produces a tremendous force, called thrust, to launch the rocket into the sky and into space.

Adding more fuel to the combustion chamber produces more thrust. This makes the

TRY FOR YOURSELF

Make a rocket

You will need:
- two straws (one thin and one thick)
- sticky tape
- plastic detergent bottle
- modeling clay
- scissors
- cardboard

1 Use sticky tape to fix the thin straw to the nozzle end of the bottle. Seal it with clay.

2 Cut out two cardboard triangles. Stick them to the end of the thick straw. Close off the other end of the straw with clay.

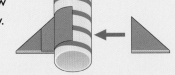

3 Slide the wide straw "rocket" over the thin straw "launcher." Squeeze the plastic bottle firmly to launch your rocket.

rocket travel faster. Stopping the fuel produces no thrust and the rocket turns off. By turning them on and off, liquid-fuel rockets can be used to steer satellites and spacecraft in space.

11

Lift Off

The rocket launch is the most dangerous part of the space mission. The rocket is full of fuel and could blow itself up.

Space rockets blast off from specially designed launchpads. The rocket needs to be upright to launch, so it is held up by a tall tower. When the engines start up, white-hot exhaust gases blast through the nozzle at the rear of the rocket. Concrete tunnels vent these hot gases away from the rocket. This is very important. The rocket is full of fuel, so it could explode in a fireball as soon as the engine started. The launch site is far away from towns and cities in case the rocket blows up and there is an accident.

Countdown

When the countdown starts, hundreds of scientists and engineers ensure everything

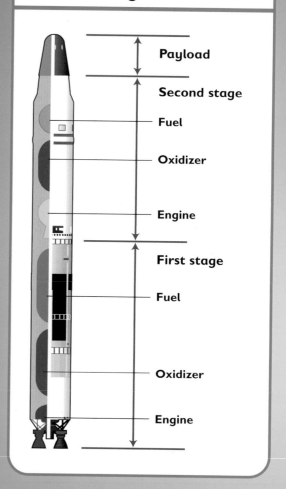

Rocket stages

- Payload
- Second stage
- Fuel
- Oxidizer
- Engine
- First stage
- Fuel
- Oxidizer
- Engine

happens at the right time. They work from Launch Control in a building near the launchpad. During the countdown, engineers fill the rocket with fuel. A day before the launch, the launch team clears the launchpad. In piloted missions, astronauts climb the tower and

Apollo 15 launches aboard the giant
Saturn V rocket on July 26, 1971.

enter the top of the rocket a
few hours before the launch.
Loudspeakers announce the
final ten seconds. The engines
fire, and the rocket blasts off
into space. Lift off!

THAT'S AMAZING!

Space rockets are made up
of many stages. When the
first stage runs out, the
next stage fires. Each stage
fires in the right order to
carry heavy payloads, such
as satellites, into space.

Satellites

Some rockets launch objects to explore planets far from Earth, but most end up circling around our planet. These objects are called satellites.

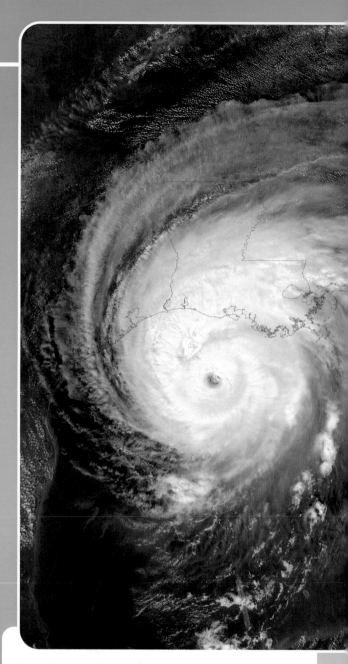

A weather satellite tracks the movement of Hurricane Rita across the Gulf of Mexico in September 2005.

Satellites have different uses. Communications satellites are used to send telephone calls, TV images, and computer signals around the world. For example, a TV transmitter might beam a live news broadcast to a communications satellite. All the pictures and sound are sent as radio waves. The satellite picks up the signals and sends them back to receivers on Earth. The signals are then sent from TV studios into people's homes.

Weather satellites

Weather satellites take pictures of Earth's atmosphere. Special cameras can measure the temperature of the air, land, and ocean. The satellites send the information to weather forecasters on Earth. They use it to predict the weather.

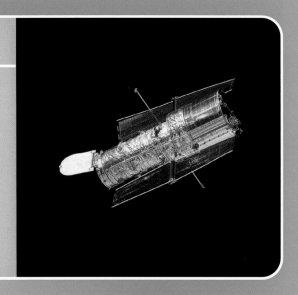

Spy satellites

Many countries around the world use satellites to spy on their enemies. The satellites take images of their enemies and beam the information back to Earth. The military uses the information to spy on enemy positions and plan attacks.

Space stations

Space stations are satellites that carry a crew. The crew do experiments and see how their bodies cope with living in space. The Soviet Union launched the largest space station, *Mir*, in 1986. It was designed to last for three years but it carried on working until 2001. It has been replaced by the International Space Station.

Astronaut Shannon Lucid trains onboard the Russian space station *Mir* in 1996.

15

Into Orbit

Satellites and other spacecraft move around Earth in a circular path called an orbit.

Changing speed

When a satellite changes its speed, it changes the height of its orbit. If it goes faster, it will move higher. If it slows down, it will move lower. Booster rockets adjust the orbit by slowing or speeding up the satellite.

Staying in orbit

If you drop an apple, it will land by your feet. Gravity pulls the apple toward the center of Earth. The same force of gravity keeps you and everything else on Earth from drifting into space.

If you throw the apple as far as you can, it will fall in a curve before it hits the ground. The harder you can throw the apple, the farther it will go before it reaches the ground.

Rockets "throw" satellites around Earth. The satellite is very high and moves quickly so it "falls" in a curve, or orbit, around the planet.

Gravity pulls
on apple

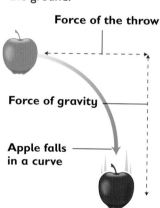

Force of the throw

Force of gravity

Apple falls
in a curve

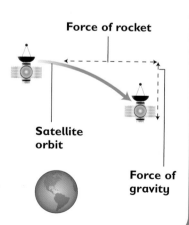

Force of rocket

Satellite
orbit

Force of
gravity

How do we use satellites?

We use man-made satellites in our everyday lives. They are used to find out what the weather will be like, to make telephone calls, to watch television, and even to spy on enemies!

Satellites orbit the Earth and record information, such as photographs of Earth's weather, from space. This information is transmitted back to the ground through an electronic signal.

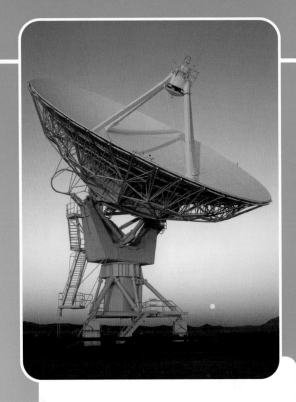

Satellite receiver dishes on Earth receive the messages sent from the satellite in space.

THAT'S AMAZING!

Communications satellites stay in orbit over the same part of the world all the time. Spy satellites orbit close to Earth to take clear pictures of the surface.

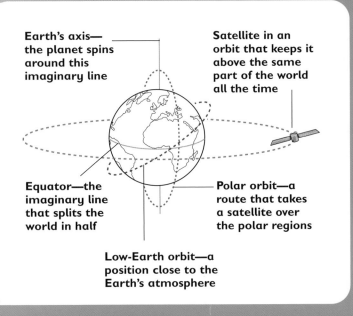

Earth's axis—the planet spins around this imaginary line

Satellite in an orbit that keeps it above the same part of the world all the time

Equator—the imaginary line that splits the world in half

Polar orbit—a route that takes a satellite over the polar regions

Low-Earth orbit—a position close to the Earth's atmosphere

Mission to the Moon

The Moon missions were born out of the space race between the United States and the Soviet Union. By landing a man on the Moon, the two countries thought that they could control space.

First, the two countries sent space probes to the Moon to check if it was safe. One Soviet probe, called *Luna 9*, made the first landing on February 3, 1966. It took pictures, studied samples of Moon rocks, and sent the data back to Earth. The *Surveyor 1* probe made the first U.S. landing on the moon four months later.

The Apollo missions

The probes showed that it was safe to land an astronaut on the Moon. NASA gave its Apollo program the go ahead. The astronauts trained in orbit aboard small spacecraft. Engineers and scientists back on Earth made sure everything was working properly.

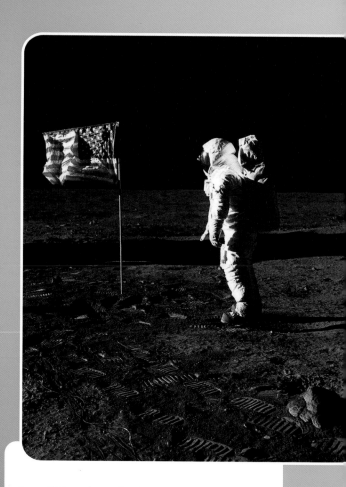

Buzz Aldrin plants the Stars and Stripes on the Moon on July 20, 1969. The Americans had won the race to the Moon with the *Apollo 11* mission.

Man on the Moon

On July 20, 1969, the *Apollo 11* mission achieved the dream of landing astronauts on the Moon. Astronauts Neil Armstrong and Edwin "Buzz" Aldrin stayed on the Moon for just a few hours. They collected Moon rocks and set up a few experiments. On later missions, the astronauts stayed much longer. The Apollo program ended in 1972. No one has been back since.

THAT'S AMAZING!

There were three main parts to the Apollo spacecraft.
- The crew lived in the Command Module.
- The Lunar Module landed on the Moon.
- The Service Module carried fuel tanks and rockets for steering.

Eugene Cernan takes a Moon buggy–the lunar rover–for a drive during the *Apollo 17* mission.

Fly me to the Moon

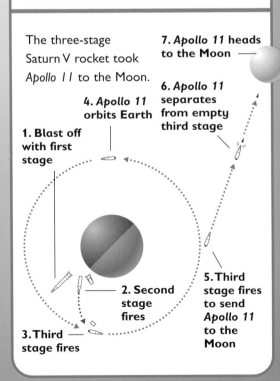

The three-stage Saturn V rocket took *Apollo 11* to the Moon.

1. Blast off with first stage

2. Second stage fires

3. Third stage fires

4. Apollo 11 orbits Earth

5. Third stage fires to send Apollo 11 to the Moon

6. Apollo 11 separates from empty third stage

7. Apollo 11 heads to the Moon

Space Shuttle

The space shuttle is the only spacecraft that can carry satellites, astronauts, and their gear into space and return them safely back to Earth.

Even before the Americans had made their historic Moon landing, they were designing a space shuttle that could return to Earth. The space shuttle program was launched in January 1972—one year after the last Moon landing by *Apollo 17*. Four years later, the first shuttle, called *Enterprise*, was completed. *Enterprise* was not capable of space flight. It was used to run tests and plan for future space shuttles.

A giant fuel tank supplies the space shuttle with liquid fuel to launch it into orbit.

Shuttle statistics

The space shuttle is made up of an orbiter, which is about the same size as a 737 passenger jet airliner—around 120 feet (37 meters) long and weighing around 50 tons (45 tonnes). The orbiter launches in two stages. Two solid-fuel rockets provide the main thrust to get the shuttle off the ground. The shuttle's own rocket engines then take over. They burn liquid fuel kept in the fuel tank. This provides the shuttle with enough power to get into orbit. When the mission is over, the shuttle re-enters the atmosphere and glides back to Earth like an airplane.

Space Shuttle *Atlantis* made its historic docking with space station *Mir* on June 25, 1995.

Fast Facts

- Atlantis, Challenger, Columbia, Discovery, *and* Endeavour *are the names of the five U.S. space shuttles.*
- *The first shuttle, Columbia, was launched in 1981.*
- *In 1986, Challenger exploded during take off, killing all seven crew members.*

Rocket Mover

Machines called crawler-transporters are used to move the space shuttle from the assembly hangars to the launch site.

Crawler-transporters are 130 feet (39 meters) long and 115 feet (34 meters) wide. The shuttle platform stands about 20 feet (6 meters) above the ground. The transporter picks up the shuttle on a special launcher platform. It then travels along a roadway that joins the assembly hangars to the launch site. The roadway is only 5 miles (8 kilometers) long, but it takes five hours to make the trip. The transporter's two diesel engines burn 750 gallons (2,850 liters) of fuel to make the trip. Most cars could travel 22,500 miles (36,000 kilometers) using the same amount of fuel.

On the right track

The transporter moves on eight continuous tracks—two on each corner of the platform. Each track is 10 feet (3 meters) high and 40 feet (12 meters) long.

The crawler-transporter carries Space Shuttle *Discovery* to Launchpad 39B at the Kennedy Space Center in Florida.

On a level

As it reaches the launch pad complex, the transporter rises up a slight ramp. A leveling system keeps the platform flat as the transporter moves up the ramp. This stops the shuttle from falling over.

The transporter's tracks are huge. A single link in the track weighs almost 1 ton (0.9 tonnes).

Fast Facts

● NASA's two crawler-transporters were built to move the Saturn V rockets to their launch sites during the Apollo missions to the Moon. Today, they carry the space shuttles to their launch sites.
● They have traveled more than 2,500 miles (4,000 km) since they were first built in the 1960s.
● The transporter's huge platform is so big a baseball diamond would fit on it.

Shuttle Launch and Landing

The space shuttle usually takes off from Kennedy Space Center in Florida and lands back at the same site.

The shuttle launches in two stages. First, two solid-fuel booster rockets fire and send the shuttle into the sky. A few minutes later, the liquid-fuel rockets take over.

Earth orbit

The shuttle orbits between 120 and 250 miles (190 and 400 kilometers) above Earth. Crew members make repairs and do their experiments as the shuttle orbits Earth.

Space Shuttle *Challenger* moves at 17,000 miles (27,400 kilometers) per hour in orbit. The cargo-bay doors have opened, ready to deploy its load.

Launch and landing sequence

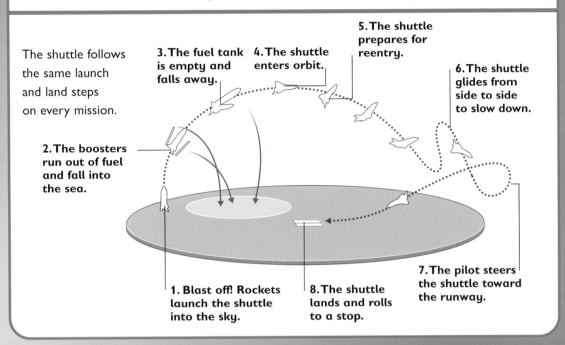

The shuttle follows the same launch and land steps on every mission.

3. The fuel tank is empty and falls away.

4. The shuttle enters orbit.

5. The shuttle prepares for reentry.

6. The shuttle glides from side to side to slow down.

2. The boosters run out of fuel and fall into the sea.

1. Blast off! Rockets launch the shuttle into the sky.

8. The shuttle lands and rolls to a stop.

7. The pilot steers the shuttle toward the runway.

Landing the shuttle

When the mission is complete, the shuttle starts the journey back to Earth. It reenters Earth's atmosphere, using rockets to slow the fall. The movement of the shuttle in the atmosphere creates friction, and the shuttle's surface gets very hot. Black tiles on the nose, tail, and underside absorb the heat. This protects the shuttle from burning up. Eventually, the shuttle glides down and lands on the runway like an airplane.

THAT'S AMAZING!

The shuttle is traveling at 220 miles (320 km) per hour as it touches down. A parachute slows it to a complete stop within 3 miles (4.5 km).

Rocket-powered Planes

Rocket-powered planes were flying through the skies long before the first rockets made it into space.

The Germans made the first rocket-powered plane, *Komet*, in World War II (1939–1945), but it was too hard to fly. In 1947, U.S. pilot Chuck Yeager (1923–) in his X-1 rocket plane became the first person to fly faster than the speed of sound—650 miles (1,040 kilometers) per hour.

Touching space

Rocket-powered planes got faster. The X-15 was one of the fastest, reaching 4,250 miles (6,800 kilometers) per hour—seven times the speed of sound. The pilots of the X-15 were flying on the edge of space—around 67 miles (107 kilometers)

THAT'S AMAZING!

Fighter pilots have small solid-fuel rockets under the seats of their aircraft. In an emergency, the pilot pulls a handle, the rockets fire, and the seat and pilot shoot out of the cockpit. The pilot can then parachute to safety.

DANGER
EJECTION
SEAT
DANGER
DANGER

above Earth's surface. They earned the name *astronauts* (from the Greek meaning "star sailor"), and it stuck. Modern fighter planes have jet engines, but a few heavy military planes still use rockets during take-off.

Rocket cars

The world land speed record was set by a jet-powered car, ThrustSSC. It traveled at 763 miles (1,228 kilometers) per hour in 1997. Richard Noble (1946–), head of the ThrustSSC team, is developing a rocket car, BloodhoundSSC. He hopes to reach 1,000 miles (1,600 kilometers) per hour.

Future of Rockets

NASA scientists are building new rockets and spacecraft to send astronauts to the Moon, and possibly even to Mars. Other countries are also joining in as space explorers.

NASA is replacing its old fleet of space shuttles. It has set up a new program called Project Constellation. There are two new Ares rockets to launch the Earth Departure Stage, Orion spacecraft, and Altair lunar lander into space. The Earth Departure Stage is a rocket that will send Orion and Altair from Earth orbit to the Moon. Orion is the crew's main spacecraft on the mission. The Altair lander will make the journey to the Moon's surface.

Life on Mars

NASA hopes to extend Project Constellation to include a Mars landing, possibly by 2037. Mars is the best hope for living on a planet other than Earth. No one could live there now. It is too cold and the air is too thin.

An artist's impression of the new Ares rocket.

An artist's impression shows Altair landing on the surface of Mars.

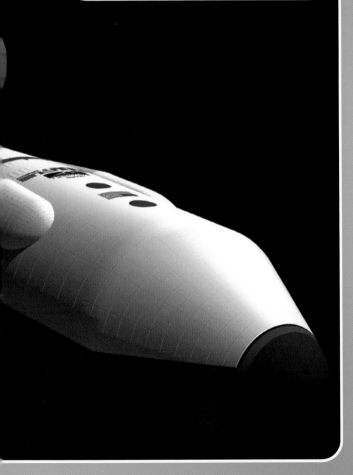

But scientists think they could warm up the planet and change the air so people could breathe, but only after hundreds of years.

A new space race

In Asia, there is a space race similar to the one between the United States and the Soviet Union in the 1960s. China, India, and Japan have all launched satellites. China already has a piloted space program. India and Japan are planning piloted missions to the Moon, too.

Glossary

astronauts: people who travel into space in a rocket and space shuttle

atmosphere: area of gas that surrounds and protects Earth

booster rockets: two large rockets on either side of a space shuttle that power the shuttle during the first two minutes of its flight

cargo: goods or materials that are carried and transported by a vehicle

combustion chamber: part of a machine or vehicle where fuel and air are mixed to create energy

engines: parts of a machine that burn fuel to make the machine move forward

exhaust: part of a machine or vehicle through which waste gases pass into the air outside

forces: pressure put upon an object to make it move or to keep it from moving

fuel: material that powers a machine, such as a rocket

gases: collections of atoms that are full of energy

gravity: the force within Earth's atmosphere that holds objects on the ground

gunpowder: explosive material

jet-powered: something that is powered forward by jet propulsion

Launch Control: place where people control and monitor the launch of a rocket

launchpad: construction from which a rocket is launched into space

liquid hydrogen: the form hydrogen takes when it is converted into a liquid. In its normal state, hydrogen is a gas.

manned: a machine or vehicle that carries people who control it

military: part of the army

nozzle: narrow tube. Materials, such as gases, can pass at speed out of a vehicle or machine.

orbit: to circle another object, such as a planet

oxidizer: one of the liquids used for rocket fuel. The oxidizer is usually liquid oxygen. It makes the other liquid burn when they are mixed together.

pressure: extreme force

radio waves: electromagnetic waves that carry sound

satellites: any object that orbits another object. Moons are satellites. Satellites are also man-made objects that are launched into space to send information back to Earth.

shuttle: machine that carries a space crew. It is transported into space by a rocket.

spacecraft: a vehicle that can travel in space

space probe: machine that travels into space to find out more about space and send information back to Earth

space race: race between United States and Russia to be the first to complete missions in space

space stations: machines that orbit the Earth and in which astronauts can study Earth and space

spacesuit: protective suit worn by an astronaut in space

transmitter: machine that can send messages as electronic signals

vent: to allow something to escape. Gases are vented away from a rocket before lift off to make sure the rocket does not explode.

Further Information

Books to read:

Bredeson, Carmen. *Liftoff!* New York, NY: Children's Press, 2003.

Gross, Miriam. *All About Space Shuttles.* New York, NY: PowerKids Press, 2009.

Web sites to look at:

www.spaceflight.nasa.gov

www.atk.com

www.boeing.com

Museums to visit:

The Franklin Institute Science Museum, Philadelphia, PA
www2.fi.edu

Kennedy Space Center, Cape Kennedy, FL
http://www.nasa.gov/centers/kennedy/home/index.html

Index